Standing Female Nude

BY CAROL ANN DUFFY

Fleshweathercock   1973
Fifth Last Song   1982

Carol Ann Duffy

Standing Female Nude

Anvil Press Poetry

Published in 1985
by Anvil Press Poetry Ltd
69 King George Street London SE10 8PX

This book is published
with financial assistance from
The Arts Council of Great Britain

Photoset in Meridien
by Bryan Williamson, Swinton, Berwickshire
Printed in Great Britain
by the Arc & Throstle Press, Todmorden, Lancs

British Library Cataloguing in Publication Data

Duffy, Carol Ann
 Standing female nude.
 I.Title
 821'.914   PR6054.U38

 ISBN 0-85646-150-4

ACKNOWLEDGEMENTS

Some of these poems have been previously published
by *Ambit*, *Aquarius*, *The Gregory Poets*, *Zip*, Rivelin
Grapheme Press, *New Directions* (USA), *The Guardian*,
The Rialto.

'Woman Seated in the Underground' was commissioned
by the Tate Gallery; 'Poem in Oils' was commissioned
by John Willett for the Horsfield exhibition in Dieppe,
1984. 'Words of Absolution' was awarded first prize in
the 1983 Greenwich International Poetry Competition;
'Whoever She Was' was awarded first prize in the 1983
National Poetry Competition.

CONTENTS

GIRL TALKING

On our Eid day my cousin was sent to
the village. Something happened. We think it was pain.
She gave wheat to the miller and the miller
gave her flour. Afterwards it did not hurt,
so for a while she made chapatis. *Tasleen,*
said her friends, *Tasleen, do come out with us.*

They were in a coy near the swing. It's like
a field. Sometimes we planted melons, spinach,
marrow, and there was a well. She sat on the swing.
They pushed her till she shouted *Stop the swing,*
then she was sick. Tasleen told them to find
help. She made blood beneath the mango tree.

Her mother held her down. She thought something
was burning her stomach. We paint our hands.
We visit. We take each other money.
Outside, the children played Jack-with-Five-Stones.
Each day she'd carried water from the well
into the Mosque. Men washed and prayed to God.

After an hour she died. Her mother cried.
They called a Holy Man. He walked from Dina
to Jhang Chak. He saw her dead, then said
She went out at noon and the ghost took her heart.
From that day we were warned not to do this.
Baarh is a small red fruit. We guard our hearts.

COMPREHENSIVE

Tutumantu is like hopscotch, Kwani-kwani is like hide-and-seek.
When my sister came back to Africa she could only speak
English. Sometimes we fought in bed because she didn't know
what I was saying. I like Africa better than England.
My mother says You will like it when we get our own house.
We talk a lot about the things we used to do
in Africa and then we are happy.

Wayne. Fourteen. Games are for kids. I support
the National Front. Paki-bashing and pulling girls'
knickers down. Dad's got his own mini-cab. We watch
the video. I Spit on Your Grave. Brilliant.
I don't suppose I'll get a job. It's all them
coming over here to work. Arsenal.

Masjid at 6 o'clock. School at 8. There was
a friendly shop selling rice. They ground it at home
to make the evening nan. Families face Mecca.
There was much more room to play than here in London.
We played in an old village. It is empty now.
We got a plane to Heathrow. People wrote to us
that everything was easy here.

It's boring. Get engaged. Probably work in Safeways
worst luck. I haven't lost it yet because I want
respect. Marlon Frederic's nice but he's a bit dark.
I like Madness. The lead singer's dead good.
My mum is bad with her nerves. She won't
let me do nothing. Michelle. It's just boring.

Ejaz. They put some sausages on my plate.
As I was going to put one in my mouth
a Moslem boy jumped on me and pulled.
The plate dropped on the floor and broke. He asked me in Urdu
if I was a Moslem. I said Yes. You shouldn't be eating this.
It's a pig's meat. So we became friends.

My sister went out with one. There was murder.
I'd like to be mates, but they're different from us.
Some of them wear turbans in class. You can't help
taking the piss. I'm going in the Army.
No choice really. When I get married
I might emigrate. A girl who can cook
with long legs. Australia sounds all right.

Some of my family are named after the Moghul emperors.
Aurangzeb, Jehangir, Batur, Humayun. I was born
thirteen years ago in Jhelum. This is a hard school.
A man came in with a milk crate. The teacher told us
to drink our milk. I didn't understand what she was saying,
so I didn't go to get any milk. I have hope and am ambitious.
At first I felt as if I was dreaming, but I wasn't.
Everything I saw was true.

ALPHABET FOR AUDEN

When the words have gone away
there is nothing left to say.

Unformed thought can never be,
what you feel is what you see,
write it down and set it free
on printed pages, © Me.
I love, you love, so does he –
long live English Poetry.
Four o'clock is time for tea,
I'll be Mother, who'll be me?

Murmur, underneath your breath,
incantations to the deaf.

Here we go again. Goody.
Art can't alter History.

Praise the language, treasure each
well-earned phrase your labours reach.

In hotels you sit and sigh,
crafting lines where others cry,

puzzled why it doesn't pay
shoving couplets round all day.
There is vodka on a tray.
Up your nose the hairs are grey.

When the words done gone it's hell
having nothing left to tell.

Pummel, punch, fondle, knead them
back again to life. Read them

when you doubt yourself and when
you doubt their function, read again.

Verse can say *I told you so*
but cannot sway the status quo

one inch. Now you get lonely,
Baby want love and love only.

In the mirror you see you.
Love you always, darling. True.

When the words have wandered far
poets patronise the bar,

understanding less and less.
Truth is anybody's guess

and Time's a clock, five of three,
mix another G and T.

Set 'em up, Joe, make that two.
Wallace Stevens thought in blue.

Words drown in a drunken sea,
dumb, they clutch at memory.

Pissed you have a double view,
something else to trouble you.

Inspiration clears the decks —
if all else fails, write of sex.

Every other word's a lie,
ain't no rainbow in the sky.

Some get lucky, die in bed,
one word stubbed in the ashtray. *Dead.*

HEAD OF ENGLISH

Today we have a poet in the class.
A real live poet with a published book.
Notice the inkstained fingers girls. Perhaps
we're going to witness verse hot from the press.
Who knows. Please show your appreciation
by clapping. Not too loud. Now

sit up straight and listen. Remember
the lesson on assonance, for not all poems,
sadly, rhyme these days. Still. Never mind.
Whispering's, as always, out of bounds —
but do feel free to raise some questions.
After all, we're paying forty pounds.

Those of you with English Second Language
see me after break. We're fortunate
to have this person in our midst.
Season of mists and so on and so forth.
I've written quite a bit of poetry myself,
am doing Kipling with the Lower Fourth.

Right. That's enough from me. On with the Muse.
Open a window at the back. We don't
want winds of change about the place.
Take notes, but don't write reams. Just an essay
on the poet's themes. Fine. Off we go.
Convince us that there's something we don't know.

Well. Really. Run along now girls. I'm sure
that gave an insight to an outside view.
Applause will do. Thank you
very much for coming here today. Lunch
in the hall? Do hang about. Unfortunately
I have to dash. Tracey will show you out.

LIZZIE, SIX

What are you doing?
I'm watching the moon.
I'll give you the moon
when I get up there.

Where are you going?
To play in the fields.
I'll give you fields,
bend over that chair.

What are you thinking?
I'm thinking of love.
I'll give you love
when I've climbed this stair.

Where are you hiding?
Deep in the wood.
I'll give you wood
when your bottom's bare.

Why are you crying?
I'm afraid of the dark.
I'll give you the dark
and I do not care.

ASH WEDNESDAY 1984

In St Austin's and Sacré Coeur the accents of ignorance
sing out. The Catholic's spanking wains are marked
by a bigot's thumbprint dipped in burnt black palm.
Dead language rises up and does them harm.

I remember this. The giving up of gobstoppers
for Lent, the weekly invention of venial sin
in a dusty box. Once, in pale blue dresses,
we kissed petals for the Bishop's feet.

Stafford's guilty sinners slobbered at their beads, beneath
the purple-shrouded plaster saints. We were Scottish,
moved down there for work, and every Sunday
I was leathered up the road to Church.

Get to Communion and none of your cheek.
We'll put the fear of God in your bones.
Swallow the Eucharist, humble and meek.
St Stephen was martyred with stones.

It makes me sick. My soul is not a vest
spattered with wee black marks. Miracles and shamrocks
and transubstantiation are all my ass.
For Christ's sake, do not send your kids to Mass.

EDUCATION FOR LEISURE

Today I am going to kill something. Anything.
I have had enough of being ignored and today
I am going to play God. It is an ordinary day,
a sort of grey with boredom stirring in the streets.

I squash a fly against the window with my thumb.
We did that at school. Shakespeare. It was in
another language and now the fly is in another language.
I breathe out talent on the glass to write my name.

I am a genius. I could be anything at all, with half
the chance. But today I am going to change the world.
Something's world. The cat avoids me. The cat
knows I am a genius and has hidden itself.

I pour the goldfish down the bog. I pull the chain.
I see that it is good. The budgie is panicking.
Once a fortnight, I walk the two miles into town
for signing on. They don't appreciate my autograph.

There is nothing left to kill. I dial the radio
and tell the man he's talking to a superstar.
He cuts me off. I get our bread-knife and go out.
The pavements glitter suddenly. I touch your arm.

I REMEMBER ME

There are not enough faces. Your own gapes back
at you on someone else, but paler, then the moment
when you see the next one and forget yourself.

It must be dreams that make us different, must be
private cells inside a common skull.
One has the other's look and has another memory.

Despair stares out from tube-trains at itself
running on the platform for the closing door. Everyone
you meet is telling wordless barefaced truths.

Sometimes the crowd yields one you put a name to,
snapping fiction into fact. Mostly your lover passes
in the rain and does not know you when you speak.

THIS SHAPE

derived from a poem by Jean Genet

This shape is a rose, protect it, it's pure.
Preserve it. Already the evening unfolds you
before me. Naked, entwined, standing
in a sheet against a wall. This shape.

My lips tremble on its delicate brim
and dare to gather the drops which fall.
Your milk swells my throat to the neck of a dove.
O stay. Rose with pearl petals, remain.

Thorny sea-fruits tear my skin. Your image
at night's end. Fingertips of smoke break surface.
My tongue thrusts, drinks at the rose's edge.
My heart uncertain. Golden hair, ghostly nape.

Destroy this anchor to impossible living, vomiting
on a sea of bile. Harnessed to your body
I move through a vast world without goodness
where you come to me only in sleep.

I roll on the ocean with you vaguely above,
working the axles, twisting through your storms.
Faraway and angry. Wanting the sky
to thread the horizon with a cloth of my stitching.

How can I sleep with this flesh that uncurls the sea?
Beautiful story of love. A village child
adores the sentry wandering on the beach.
My amber hand draws in a boy of iron.

Sleeper, your body. This shape, extraordinary.
Creamy almond, star, o curled up child.
A tingling stir of blood in the blue departure
of evening. A naked foot sounding on the grass.

SAYING SOMETHING

Things assume your shape; discarded clothes, a damp shroud
in the bathroom, vacant hands. This is not fiction. This is
the plain and warm material of love. My heart assumes it.

We wake. Our private language starts the day. We make
familiar movements through the house. The dreams we have
no phrases for slip through our fingers into smoke.

I dreamed I was not with you. Wandering in a city
where you did not live, I stared at strangers, searching
for a word to make them you. I woke beside you.

Sweetheart, I say. Pedestrian daylight terms scratch
darker surfaces. Your absence leaves me with the ghost
of love; half-warm coffee cups or sheets, the gentlest kiss.

Walking home, I see you turning on the lights. I come in
from outside calling your name, saying something.

JEALOUS AS HELL

Blind black shark swim in me,
move to possess. Slow stupid shape
grin in sea, suck inky on suspicions.
Swim grin suck, it clot my heart.

Big fish brooding in the water.
Bright bird buoyant in the sky.

Tail-shudder thrust wounded, it
ugly from imaginary pains. Bones
of contention rot in gut. Mouth open
shut open shut open. Hateshark coming.

Big fish smoulder for the slaughter.
Clever wings fly small bird high.

Evilbreath lurk at base of spine,
seethe sightless from heart to mind.
Devilteeth, sack of greed, reasonless.
It will kill. Swim grin suck.

Bird skim surface of the ocean.
Fish churn clumsy in the sea.

It wait in the gurgling dark.
Bad shark. Blue belly blubber
wanting bird. Sick with lust
it flick its great tail, it flick.

Freedom bird glide in its own motion.
Shark need nothing to be free.

It watch you every move.

TERZA RIMA SW19

Over this Common a kestrel treads air
till the earth says *mouse* or *vole*. Far below
two lovers walking by the pond seem unaware.

She feeds the ducks. He wants her, tells her so
as she half-smiles and stands slightly apart.
He loves me, loves me not with each deft throw.

It could last a year, she thinks, possibly two
and then crumble like stale bread. The kestrel flies
across the sun as he swears his love is true

and, darling, forever. Suddenly the earth cries
Now and death drops from above like a stone.
A couple turn and see a strange bird rise.

Into the sky a kestrel climbs alone
and later she might write or he may phone.

NAMING PARTS

A body has been discussed between them.
The woman wears a bruise
upon her arm. Do not wear your heart
upon your sleeve, he cautions, knowing
which part of whom has caused the injury.
Underneath the lamplight you teach me new games
with a wicked pack of cards. I am
the Jack of Diamonds and, for this trick only,
you my Queen. Beware the Ace of Spades.

Her heart is broken and he fears his liver
will explode. Outside the world whimpers
and rumours bite like gnats in bloodless ears.
You have placed my small hand on your large penis.
This is an erection. This is the life. This
is another fine mess. Perhaps soup will comfort them.
To have only soup against such sorrow.
I cannot bear alone and watch
my hands reach sadly for the telephone.

Once someone asked if she was hurting him
and once a wonderful lass destroyed him
with a kiss. You've given me the benefit of your doubt.
We forgive them nothing. I want
a better part than this. He shuffles the pack
and tells her to wait. She thinks of the loved body
talked of like weather. She's putting the ingredients
into the soup he likes. It's true or none of it's true.
Someone is cared for who is past caring. Somewhere.

TILL OUR FACE

Whispers weave webs amongst thighs. I open
like the reddest fruit. Between the rapid spaces
of the rain the world sweats seas and damp
strings tremble for a perfect sound.

A bow tugs catgut. Something inside me
steps on a highwire where you search crimson
for a silver thread. A rose glows beneath
the drift of pine needles. I bite your lip, lost.

Come further in, where eyes stare inward
at the skull as the roof of the brain
takes flight. Your mouth laps petals till our face
is a flower soaked in its own scent.

The planets abandon us.

LOVEBIRDS

I wait for your step.
A jay on the cherry tree
trembles the blossom.

I name you *my love*
and the gulls fly above us
calling to the air.

Our two pale bodies
move in the late light, slowly
as doves do, breathing.

And then you are gone.
A night-owl mourns in darkness
for the moon's last phase.

old lovers die hard, as in the restaurant
we pass the bread between us like a symbol
of betrayal. One of you tonight.
The habits are the same, small intimacies
flaring up across the table. They've placed
a candle in the middle over which
we carefully avoid our history.

How do you sleep? Something corny
like Our Song pipes out. I know
you're still too mean to pay the bill.
Our new loves sit beside us guardedly,
outside the private jokes. I think
of all the tediousness of loss but, yes,
I'm happy now. Yes. Happy. Now.

Darling, whatever it was that covered
such an ordinary form with light
has long since gone. It is a candle
shapes the memory. Perhaps the wine.
I see our gestures endlessly repeated as
you turn to yours the way you used
to turn to me. I turn to mine. And

FREE WILL

The country in her heart babbled a language
she couldn't explain. When she had found the money
she paid them to take something away from her.
Whatever it was she did not permit it a name.

It was nothing yet she found herself grieving nothing.
Beyond reason her body mourned, though the mind
counselled like a doctor who had heard it all before.
When words insisted they were silenced with a cigarette.

Dreams were a nightmare. Things she did not like
to think about persisted in being thought.
They were in her blood, bobbing like flotsam;
as sleep retreated they were strewn across her face.

Once, when small, she sliced a worm in half,
gazing as it twinned beneath the knife.
What she parted would not die despite
the cut, remained inside her all her life.

ALLIANCE

What she has retained of herself is a hidden grip
working her face like a glove-puppet. She smiles
at his bullying, this Englishman who talks scathingly
of *Frogs* in front of his French wife.

She is word-perfect. Over the years he has inflated
with best bitter till she has no room. *Je t'aime*
isn't in it. One morning she awoke to a foreigner
lying beside her and her heart slammed shut.

The youngest lives at home. She stays up late
to feed what keeps her with the father. England
ruined him and holds her hostage in the garden,
thinking of her sons and what they've cost.

Or dreaming in another language with a different name
about a holiday next year. He staggers in half-pissed
and plonks his weight down on her life, hates her
for whatever reason she no longer lets him near.

A CLEAR NOTE

1 AGATHA

Eight children to feed, I worked as a nurse
tending the dying. Four kids to each breast.
You can see from the photographs
my long auburn hair.

Kiss me goodnight – me weeping in our bed.
The scunner would turn away cold, back rigid,
but come home from work and take me on the floor
with his boots on and his blue eyes shut.

Moll, all my life I wanted the fields of Ireland only
and a man to delight in me
who'd never be finished with kisses and say
Look at the moon. My darling. The moon.

Instead, a move across the water
to Glasgow and long years of loathing
with the devil I'd married. I felt love freeze
to a fine splinter in my heart.

Again and again throwing life from my loins
like a spider with enough rope
spinning and wringing its own neck. And he
wouldn't so much as hold me after the act.

It won't be over till one of us is dead.
Out there in the streets there's a corpse
walking round in a good suit and a trilby.
Don't bury him on top of me. Please.

I had a voice once, but it's broken
and cannot recall the unspoken words
I tried to whisper in his closed ear.
Look at the moon. My darling. The moon.

Who'd have thought to die alone on the telephone
wheezing at strangers? The snowqueen's heart
stopping forever and melting as it stopped.
Once I was glorious with a new frock and high hopes.

Is it mad to dream then? What a price
to pay. But when hair bled colour
and the starved body began eating itself,
I had forgotten how to dream.

What laughs, Moll, for you and me
to swim in impossible seas. You've a daughter
yourself now to talk through the night.
I was famous for my hats. Remember.

Workmen whistled as I stepped out,
although I ignored them. I had pride. Remember
my fine hair and my smart stride
in the park with the eight of you spruced.

Please. From behind silence I ask
for an epitaph of light. Let some imagine.
Bernadette, little grandchild, one day
you must tell them I wanted the moon. *Yes*.

2   MOLL

Some hurts pass, pet, but others
lurk on. They turn up
like old photos and catch at the throat
somehow. I'm forty-nine in May.

Her death haunts me, almost
as I haunted her womb and you mine.
A presence inside me which will neither grow
nor diminish. What can a woman do?

The job pays well, but more than that
there's the freedom. Your father's against it.
He loves me as much now as he did
twenty-five years ago. More.

Sometimes I think I'll walk out the door
and keep right on walking. But then
there's the dinner to cook. I take her flowers
every year and talk to the tombstone.

You were a wild wain, with an answer
for everything. Near killed me containing you.
Boys are different. I can read you
like a book, like the back of my hand.

They call me Madcap Moll. I'd love to leap
on a bike and ride to the seaside
alone. There's something out there
that's passing me by. Are you following me?

I've been drained since twenty, but not empty
yet. I roam inside myself, have
such visions you'd not credit. The best times
are daydreams with a cigarette.

There was that night, drunk, I told you
Never have kids. Give birth to yourself,
I wish I had. And your Dad, looking daggers
stormed off to bed. Laugh? I cried.

I can't fly out to stay with you alone,
there'd be fights for a month.
He broods on what I'd get up to
given half the chance. Men!

Hardest to bear is knowing my own strength.
Does that sound strange? Yet four daft sons
and a husband handle me like gold leaf.
Me, with a black hole of resources.

Over and over again as a child
you'd be at me to sing
The stars at night are big and bright.
Aye. So still they are.

Here's me blethering on. What laughs,
Bernadette, for us to swim in impossible seas
under the moon. Let's away, my darling,
for a good long walk. And I'll tell you a secret.

3   BERNADETTE

The day her mother died, my mother
was on holiday. I travelled to the seaside
with bad news. She slumped over the table,
spilling wine across the telegram.

Someone burnt the diary she wrote. It was
a catalogue of hatred and it was all
she had to leave. Extracts were whispered
at the wake and then it was forgotten.

Her mouth was set as though she was angry.
Kiss me goodnight. My mother went in.
She saw him bend over the coffin to kiss her
and half-thought the corpse had flinched.

I can't remember much. Perhaps the smell
of my granny mingling with hers
in a gossipy bed. Them giggling. One sang
Hang down your head Tom Dooley in the dark.

Or assuming a virtuous expression
so they'd let you stay up late. Listening
as language barely stretched to cover
what remained unsaid.

They buried him on top within the month.
I don't want that bastard
rotting above me for all eternity.
What does it matter, they said, now she's dead?

Can't see the moon now, Moll.
Listen. The hopes of your thousand mothers
sing with a clear note inside you.
Away, while you can, and travel the world.

I can almost hear her saying it now.
Who will remember me? Bleak decades of silence
and lovelessness placing her years away
from the things that seem natural to us.

For we swim with ease in all
possible seas and do not forget them.
It's spring again and just about now
my Granny would be buying a new hat.

And I have hair like hers. My mother
is setting off for work. An aeroplane
climbs up above her house. She imagines me
seeing it from my window later on.

As I imagine the simplest thing. The dreams
of women which will harm no one.
April in the graveyard sees new flowers
pushing out from the old earth.

The daylight disappears. Against the night
a plane's lights come from somewhere else. For Moll
the life goes streaming back in tune.
For Agatha, from Bernadette, the moon.

WORDS OF ABSOLUTION

She clings to life by a rosary,
ninety years old. Who made you?
God made me. Pearl died a bairn
and him blacklisted. Listen
to the patterns of your prayers
down the years. What is Purgatory?

The guilt and stain of Original Sin.
Except the Virgin. Never a drink
or tobacco and the legs opened only
for childbirth. Forgive me. With her
they pass the parcel. Don't let the music
stop and me holding it. What do you mean
by the resurrection of the body?

Blessed art thou among women even if
we put you in a home. Only the silent motion
of lips and the fingering of decades.
How do we show that we love God?
Never a slack shilling, but good broth
always on the table. Which are the fasting days?
Mary Wallace, what are the days of abstinence?

Chrism, ash, holy water, beads
waiting for the end of nothing. Granny,
I have committed the Sin of Sodom.
How are we to love one another?
What are the four last things
to be ever remembered? I go to my reward.
Chastity. Piety. Modesty. Longanimity.
How should you finish the day? After
your night prayers what should you do?

DEBT

He was all night sleepless over money.
Impossible scenarios danced in the dark
as though he was drunk. The woman
stirred, a soft spoon, and what had emerged
from them dreamed in the next room, safe.
He left himself and drew a gun he didn't own.

He won the pools; pearls for her and ponies
for the kids. The damp bedroom was an ocean-liner
till the woman farted, drifted on, away from him.
Despair formed a useless prayer and worry an ulcer.
He bargained with something he could not believe in
for something he could not have. *Sir...*

Through the wallpaper men in suits appeared.
They wanted the video, wanted the furniture.
They wanted the children. Sweat soured in nylon sheets
as his heartbeat panicked, trying to get out.
There was nothing he would not do. There was
nothing to do but run the mind's mad films.

Dear Sir... his ghost typed on. He remembered
waiting for her, years ago, on pay-day
with a bar of fruit-and-nut. Somehow consoled
he reached out, found her, and then slept.
Add this. Take that away. The long night leaked
cold light into the house. A letter came.

YOU JANE

At night I fart a guinness smell against the wife
who snuggles up to me after I've given her one
after the Dog and Fox. It's all muscle. You can punch
my gut and wait forever till I flinch. Try it.
Man of the house. Master in my own home. Solid.

Look at that bicep. Dinner on the table
and a clean shirt, but I respect her point of view.
She's borne me two in eight years, knows
when to button it. Although she's run a bit to fat
she still bends over of a weekend in suspenders.

This is the life. Australia next year and bugger
the mother-in-law. Just feel those thighs.
Karate keeps me like granite. Strength of an ox.
I can cope with the ale no problem. Pints
with the lads, a laugh, then home to her.

She says Did you dream, love? I never
dream. Sleep is as black as a good jar.
I wake half-conscious with a hard-on, shove it in.
She don't complain. When I feel, I feel here
where the purple vein in my neck throbs.

WHOEVER SHE WAS

They see me always as a flickering figure
on a shilling screen. Not real. My hands,
still wet, sprout wooden pegs. I smell the apples
burning as I hang the washing out.
Mummy, say the little voices of the ghosts
of children on the telephone. Mummy.

A row of paper dollies, cleaning wounds
or boiling eggs for soldiers. The chant
of magic words repeatedly. I do not know.
Perhaps tomorrow. If we're very good.
The film is on a loop. Six silly ladies
torn in half by baby fists. When they
think of me, I'm bending over them at night
to kiss. Perfume. Rustle of silk. Sleep tight.

Where does it hurt? A scrap of echo clings
to the bramble bush. My maiden name
sounds wrong. This was the playroom.
I turn it over on a clumsy tongue. Again.
These are the photographs. Making masks
from turnips in the candlelight. In case they come.

Whoever she was, forever their wide eyes watch her
as she shapes a church and steeple in the air.
She cannot be myself and yet I have a box
of dusty presents to confirm that she was here.
You remember the little things. Telling stories
or pretending to be strong. Mummy's never wrong.
You open your dead eyes to look in the mirror
which they are holding to your mouth.

HUMAN INTEREST

Fifteen years minimum, banged up inside
for what took thirty seconds to complete.
She turned away. I stabbed. I felt this heat
burn through my skull until reason had died.

I'd slogged my guts out for her, but she lied
when I knew different. She used to meet
some prick after work. She stank of deceit.

I loved her. When I accused her, she cried
and denied it. Straight up, she tore me apart.
On the Monday, I found the other bloke
had bought her a chain with a silver heart.

When I think about her now, I near choke
with grief. My baby. She wasn't a tart
or nothing. I wouldn't harm a fly, no joke.

DREAMING OF SOMEWHERE ELSE

Those strange stone birds are smashed
on heroin. It's like the ballroom
of the frigging Titanic up here. Our friend
says nothing will happen there, ever; drinks
steadily as mortgaged dust piles up.
His cat is off its cake. *Know what I mean like?*

Long dark streets of black eternal rain
leading to nowhere. *Paris of the North this.*
Everyone's had everyone else, at least
twice. Lethal cocktails brim with revelation
and gossip. I am here to tell you
that the Cathedrals are lucky to be alive.

Behave yourself. The glass shattered, pierced
just above his eye. Laugh? He was in
stitches. Even the river is too pissed
to go anywhere; it stares upwards at stars
reflecting a hungover moon for doomed lovers.
Et in Arcadia Ego and in the Philharmonic.

Nerves of steel you need in this game
as the wind screams up from the Pier Head
dragging desolation, memory; as the orchestra
plays on for the last dancers bouncing off the walls.
Somewhere else another universe takes light years
to be seen even though it went out already. *You wha'?*

BEFORE YOU JUMP

for Mister Berryman

Tell us what these tough words have done
to you.

       I demand Love and Attention now
with my little fists, with the muscles
of a poem. *These songs*
are not meant to be understood, you understand.
They are meant only to terrify & comfort.

Let light come daily where I grapple with
my tiny tasks. The golden beehive
brims with honey as the bees collapse.
That much for little sweetness, yet they
fondle sculpture like a pound of flesh.
Eloi Eloi lama sabachthani.
And who shall love properly?

                You must
or we die. Walk through the churchyard
past the crocuses. They won't last long.
My guardian angel has abandoned me but soon
we'll fly upon the curve of earth.
A miracle is all I ask. Not much.
The red wet mouth cries out that jealousy
was ruin of them all.   Save me.

Or manage with a flab of language
breaking back for fitness. And alone. If in the evening
someone wanders in with open arms
we will be blessed. If one says Yes.
I mean always what I say. Listen.
Do you mean what you say?

In slow motion he is falling, spinning
down forever. Pray for us now.
Unless there was one voice. Faithfulness.
Unless that were possible. Patience.
There must be only me. For this
I'll give myself, even my breath.
But say we are not lost. Darling.
A man crimson with need and getting nothing.

The tongue licks in and out and Look
what I can do. Fame and Money better never
than too late. Let this cup pass me by.
They're killing me; the images, the sounds
of what is in this world. You turn away
repeatedly. You always turn away.

From jewels and garbage I have fashioned
marvellous machines, but am of little matter
in the end. No more to say. I disbelieve
in everything whilst nothing speaks.
Climb down from there and come into the warm.
Forever come into the warm. Unless there were
one voice. Unless I thought it possible there were.

A PROVINCIAL PARTY, 1956

A chemical inside you secretes the ingredients of fear.
Is it fear? You know for sure you feel
uneasy on that black, plastic sofa, even though
the ice melts in a long tumbler behind red triangles.
You don't find it sexy, your first blue movie
in a stranger's flat, but you watch it anyway.

Embarrassment crackles like three petticoats. You never
imagined, married two years and all. A woman
cackles a joke you don't understand, but you laugh anyway.
On one stocking, you have halted a ladder
with clear varnish. There are things going on
on the screen which would turn your Mam to salt.

Suddenly, the whole room is breathing. Someone hums
Magic Moments and then desists, moist lips apart.
Two men in the film are up to no good. *Christ.*
You could die with the shame. The chrome ashtray
is filled with fag-ends, lipstick-rimmed. Your suspenders
pinch you spitefully, like kids nipping spoilsports.

You daren't look, but something is happening
on the Cyril Lord. Part of you tells yourself it's only
shaving-cream. You and him do it with the light off.
This will give him ideas. It *is* fear. You nudge and nudge
till your husband squirms away from you and smiles
at the young, male host with film-star eyes.

DEAR NORMAN

I have turned the newspaper boy into a diver
for pearls. I can do this. In my night
there is no moon, and if it happens that I speak
of stars it's by mistake. Or if it happens
that I mention these things, it's by design.

His body is brown, breaking through waves. Such white teeth.
Beneath the water he searches for the perfect shell.
He does not know that, as he posts The Mirror
through the door, he is equal with dolphins.
I shall name him Pablo, because I can.

Pablo laughs and shakes the seaweed from his hair.
Translucent on his palm a pearl appears. He is reminded.
Cuerpo de mujer, blancas colinas, muslos blancos.
I find this difficult, and then again easy,
as I watch him push his bike off in the rain.

As I watch him push his bike off in the rain
I trace his name upon the window-pane.
There is little to communicate, but I have re-arranged
the order of the words. Pablo says You want for me
to dive again? I want for you to dive.

Tomorrow I shall deal with the dustman.

TALENT

This is the word *tightrope*. Now imagine
a man, inching across it in the space
between our thoughts. He holds our breath.

There is no word *net*.

You want him to fall, don't you?
I guessed as much; he teeters but succeeds.
The word *applause* is written all over him.

$

A one a two a one two three four –
boogie woogie chou chou cha cha chatta
noogie. Woogie wop a loo bop a wop
bim bam. Da doo ron a doo ron oo wop a
sha na? Na na hey hey doo wah did.
Um, didy ay didy shala lala lala lala,
boogie woogie choo choo cha cha bop.
(A woogie wop a loo bam) yeah yeah yeah.

LIVERPOOL ECHO

Pat Hodges kissed you once, although quite shy,
in sixty-two. Small crowds in Matthew Street
endure rain for the echo of a beat,
as if nostalgia means you did not die.

Inside phone-booths loveless ladies cry
on Merseyside. Their faces show defeat.
An ancient jukebox blares out Ain't She Sweet
in Liverpool, which cannot say goodbye.

Here everybody has an anecdote
of how they met you, were the best of mates.
The seagulls circle round a ferry-boat

out on the river, where it's getting late.
Like litter on the water, people float
outside the Cavern in the rain. And wait.

BACK DESK

I am Franz Schubert of Dresden. It was not easy.
Quite soon I realised my prowess on the violin
was mediocre, but we had to eat.
The piece I wrote (The Bee, you may remember it)
paid for that winter's clothing, little else.
The children danced in their new clogs
till the strings snapped on the highest note.
I saw him once in Heidelberg, the other Franz.
He was older than I, seemed younger.
Smaller than I, looked taller.

STANDING FEMALE NUDE

Six hours like this for a few francs.
Belly nipple arse in the window light,
he drains the colour from me. Further to the right,
Madame. And do try to be still.
I shall be represented analytically and hung
in great museums. The bourgeoisie will coo
at such an image of a river-whore. They call it Art.

Maybe. He is concerned with volume, space.
I with the next meal. You're getting thin,
Madame, this is not good. My breasts hang
slightly low, the studio is cold. In the tea-leaves
I can see the Queen of England gazing
on my shape. Magnificent, she murmurs
moving on. It makes me laugh. His name

is Georges. They tell me he's a genius.
There are times he does not concentrate
and stiffens for my warmth. Men think of their mothers.
He possesses me on canvas as he dips the brush
repeatedly into the paint. Little man,
you've not the money for the arts I sell.
Both poor, we make our living how we can.

I ask him Why do you do this? Because
I have to. There's no choice. Don't talk.
My smile confuses him. These artists
take themselves too seriously. At night I fill myself
with wine and dance around the bars. When it's finished
he shows me proudly, lights a cigarette. I say
Twelve francs and get my shawl. It does not look like me.

POEM IN OILS

What I have learnt I have learnt from the air,
from infinite varieties of light. Muted colours
alter gradually as clouds stir shape, till purple rain
or violet thunderstorm shudders in the corner of my eye.

Here, on this other coast, the motifs multiply.
I hesitate before the love the waves bear
to the earth. Is this what I see?
No, but this is the process of seeing.

Believe me, soundless shadows fall from trees
like brushstrokes. A painter stands
upon a cliff and turns doubt into certainty where,
far below, the ocean fills itself with sky.

I was here to do this. And was curious.

OPPENHEIM'S CUP AND SAUCER

She asked me to luncheon in fur. Far from
the loud laughter of men, our secret life stirred.

I remember her eyes, the slim rope of her spine.
This is your cup, she whispered, and this mine.

We drank the sweet hot liquid and talked dirty.
As she undressed me, her breasts were a mirror

and there were mirrors in the bed. She said Place
your legs around my neck, that's right. Yes.

INK ON PAPER

COMPOSITION 1

The heart is placid. The wireless makes
a slow movement to shape the invisible.
On the table, apples imitate an old motif;
beyond them, through the window, gulls applaud
the trees. Something has happened. Clouds
move away, superior and bored. A cigarette
fumes in a brown clay ashtray, ignored.

COMPOSITION 2

A dark red armchair with no one in it
waits patiently. Empty wet wellingtons
warm ghost-legs at the gas fire. There is
the sound of a woman's voice crying
on the other side of the door and the smell
of onions frying. Beneath the chair, an umbrella
half-exists. Behind the curtains, glass, rain.

COMPOSITION 3

This bowl of fruit obstinately refuses
to speak the language. Pink vain peaches
remain aloof in late light. The grapefruit
will only be yellow as long as anyone looks.
In the other bowl, two goldfish try harder.
Unwatched, the man watches the cat, watching.
An orange is more still than the near-silence.

WOMAN SEATED IN
THE UNDERGROUND, 1941

after the drawing by Henry Moore

I forget. I have looked at the other faces and found
no memory, no love. *Christ, she's a rum one.*
Their laughter fills the tunnel, but it does not
comfort me. There was a bang and then
I was running with the rest through smoke. Thick, grey
smoke has covered thirty years at least.
I know I am pregnant, but I do not know my name.

Now they are singing. *Underneath the lantern
by the barrack gate.* But waiting for whom?
Did I? I have no wedding ring, no handbag, nothing.
I want a fag. I have either lost my ring or I am
a loose woman. No. Someone has loved me. Someone
is looking for me even now. I live somewhere.
I sing the word *darling* and it yields nothing.

Nothing. A child is crying. Mine doesn't show yet.
Baby. My hands mime the memory of knitting.
Purl. Plain. I know how to do these things, yet my mind
has unravelled into thin threads that lead nowhere.
In a moment, I shall stand up and scream until
somebody helps me. The skies were filled with sirens, planes,
fire, bombs, and I lost myself in the crowd. Dear God.

WAR PHOTOGRAPHER

In his darkroom he is finally alone
with spools of suffering set out in ordered rows.
The only light is red and softly glows,
as though this were a church and he
a priest preparing to intone a Mass.
Belfast. Beirut. Phnom Penh. All flesh is grass.

He has a job to do. Solutions slop in trays
beneath his hands which did not tremble then
though seem to now. Rural England. Home again
to ordinary pain which simple weather can dispel,
to fields which don't explode beneath the feet
of running children in a nightmare heat.

Something is happening. A stranger's features
faintly start to twist before his eyes,
a half-formed ghost. He remembers the cries
of this man's wife, how he sought approval
without words to do what someone must
and how the blood stained into foreign dust.

A hundred agonies in black-and-white
from which his editor will pick out five or six
for Sunday's supplement. The reader's eyeballs prick
with tears between the bath and pre-lunch beers.
From the aeroplane he stares impassively at where
he earns his living and they do not care.

WHAT PRICE?

These were his diaries. Through the writing we may find
the man and whether he has been misjudged.
Admit it, even now, most people secretly resent
the Jews. We have all evening to peruse
the truth. Outside the window summer blossom falls.

It takes me back. I always saw some sense
in what he tried to do. This country should be strong.
I'll put some Wagner on the gramophone
then we can settle down. On nights like this
it makes one glad to be alive. *My own Lili Marlene.*

Of course, one had to fight. I had a wife.
But somewhere here I think you'll find
that he'd have joined with us. More wine?
I know the Sons of David died, some say atrociously,
but that's all past. The roses are in bloom.

Look at the way we claimed the islands back.
My grandchildren are young and pink
and make me proud. She has the right idea.
These journals will be his chance to explain,
I'm certainly convinced that they are real.

Not that he didn't make mistakes, but we can learn
from him. See by the larch tree how the sun goes down.
And notice all the interest from newspapers, so soon!
I admit that it was hell to be a Jew, but how much
do you think they'll fetch? One million? Two?

MISSILE

The cat is itself.
Let us consider the cauliflower,
it means no harm.
Grass is grass grows grass.
Spider spins spider. Is a rose.
Everything's only itself. Grows.

Except you, Daddy.

Birds are simple.
Wings flap fly being birds.
Feathers in the sky saying bird.
Flickers in the sea saying fish.
Bird fish stone chant name,
we show no difference, we're the same.

Except you, Daddy.

Daffodil yellow with flower
stains light. Light leaks from sun
till night. Artichoke and mushroom
shift cycle till stop. Damp loam
humming at the moon. Eyes water
at the little onions. See.

Except you, Daddy.

Oranges and lemons singing singing
buttercups and daisies. Bang.
Will ye no come back again?
My true love. Bang. Two turtle doves.
Bang. The cat is spider is grass
is roses is bird fish bang.

Bang. Bang.
Except you, Daddy.

POKER IN THE FALKLANDS
WITH HENRY & JIM

We three play poker whilst outside *the real world*
shrinks to a joker. So. Someone
deals me a queen, face up, and the bets roll.
I keep a straight face up my sleeve and peep
at the ace in the hole. Opposite me

the bearded poet raises on two kings. *In my country*
we do this. But my country sends giant
underwater tanks to massacre and I have
another queen. The queens are in love
with each other and spurn kings, diamonds
or not. A quiet man coughs and deals. Wheels

within wheels within worlds without words.
I get a second ace and raise
my eyebrows imperceptibly. A submarine drones on
amongst dolphins. Fifty and raise you fifty
for *the final card*. The cat is nervous as

Henry tells me any second the room could explode
and we would not know. Jim has three jacks
but I have three queens, two aces and a full house.
Perhaps any moment my full house might explode
though I will not know. Remember
one of us is just about to win. God.
God this is an awful game.

BORROWED MEMORY

He remembers running to the nets, in early summer,
in his cricket whites. Then there's a blur
until he's at high tea, with Harry Wharton and the rest,
in Study No. 5. What larks they had, what fun
the long terms were.

                        She remembers skating on the pond
and how she laughed when Jo and Laurie slipped
upon the ice. A Christmas tree. Sitting by the fire
whilst sipping hot rum punch. But sleepy,
so the picture's not quite clear.

                        Or was it
at a midnight feast? A bite of sardine sandwich,
then of cake until you felt quite ill. He's positive
he won the rugger prize, can see the fellows' faces
as they cheered him on.

                        On their shelves
the honour of the school has gathered dust.
These fictions are as much a part of them
as fact, for if you said *Are you quite sure
of this*? they would insist.

                        As, watching demonstrations
on the box, they see themselves in shelters by the candlelight,
with tons of tuck to see them through. Fair Play Bob
and Good Egg Sue have nursed their fantasies for years.
And they will make them true.

SHOOTING STARS

After I no longer speak they break our fingers
to salvage my wedding ring. Rebecca Rachel Ruth
Aaron Emmanuel David, stars on all our brows
beneath the gaze of men with guns. Mourn for the daughters,

upright as statues, brave. You would not look at me.
You waited for the bullet. Fell. I say Remember.
Remember these appalling days which make the world
forever bad. One saw I was alive. Loosened

his belt. My bowels opened in a ragged gape of fear.
Between the gap of corpses I could see a child.
The soldiers laughed. Only a matter of days separate
this from acts of torture now. They shot her in the eye.

How would you prepare to die, on a perfect April evening
with young men gossiping and smoking by the graves?
My bare feet felt the earth and urine trickled
down my legs until I heard the click. Not yet. A trick.

After immense suffering someone takes tea on the lawn.
After the terrible moans a boy washes his uniform.
After the history lesson children run to their toys the world
turns in its sleep the spades shovel soil Sara Ezra...

Sister, if seas part us do you not consider me?
Tell them I sang the ancient psalms at dusk
inside the wire and strong men wept. Turn thee
unto me with mercy, for I am desolate and lost.

THE B MOVIE

At a preview of That Hagen Story *in 1947, when actor*
Ronald Reagan became the first person on screen to say
"I love you, will you marry me?" to the nineteen-year-old
Shirley Temple, there was such a cry of "Oh, no!"
from the invited audience that the scene was cut out
when the film was released.

Lap dissolve. You make a man speak crap dialogue,
one day he'll make you eat your words. OK?
Let's go for a take. Where's the rest of me? *"Oh, no!"*

Things are different now. He's got star billing,
star wars, applause. Takes her in his arms.
I'm talking about a *real* weepie. Freeze frame. *"Oh, no!"*

On his say-so, the train wipes out the heroine
and there ain't no final reel. How do you like that?
My fellow Americans, we got five minutes. *"Oh, no!"*

Classic. He holds the onion to water such sorrow.
We need a Kleenex the size of Russia here, no kidding.
Have that kid's tail any time he wants to. *Yup.*

THE DOLPHINS

World is what you swim in, or dance, it is simple.
We are in our element but we are not free.
Outside this world you cannot breathe for long.
The other has my shape. The other's movement
forms my thoughts. And also mine. There is a man
and there are hoops. There is a constant flowing guilt.

We have found no truth in these waters,
no explanations tremble on our flesh.
We were blessed and now we are not blessed.
After travelling such space for days we began
to translate. It was the same space. It is
the same space always and above it is the man.

And now we are no longer blessed, for the world
will not deepen to dream in. The other knows
and out of love reflects me for myself.
We see our silver skin flash by like memory
of somewhere else. There is a coloured ball
we have to balance till the man has disappeared.

The moon has disappeared. We circle well-worn grooves
of water on a single note. Music of loss forever
from the other's heart which turns my own to stone.
There is a plastic toy. There is no hope. We sink
to the limits of this pool until the whistle blows.
There is a man and our mind knows we will die here.

SOMEONE ELSE'S DAUGHTER

Scratching at the air *(There's nothing there)*
she is snowing constantly, coming to bits, she chips
at her smooth, white arms with needles. Her kitten laps
at a glass of cold blood and stares reproachfully
straight to the centre of her pinned blue eyes.

Beneath the skin, small volcanoes sigh and draw in fire.
She covers them with make-up, itches, slopes out.
Herpes and hepatitis set off on their journey
from the mind to elsewhere. No Surrender.
Cunt and liver erupt as the thin hand shoplifts.

On the wall of the waiting-room a snake eats itself,
tail first. This is your last chance. *I know.*
Why do you do this? *I don't know.* She smokes
a trembling chain of cancer cells. She devours everything.
She drains the listener. She is eating herself tail first.

One day there will be nothing left for those
who love her. She will shrink to a childhood snapshot
as someone else's daughter moves into the squat.
She will shrink to an earlier memory. A child
gobbling so many Easter eggs she was sick for a week.

A HEALTHY MEAL

The gourmet tastes the secret dreams of cows
tossed lightly in garlic. Behind the green door, swish
of oxtails languish on an earthen dish. Here are
wishbones and pinkies; fingerbowls will absolve guilt.

Capped teeth chatter to a kidney or at the breast
of something which once flew. These hearts knew
no love and on their beds of saffron rice they lie
beyond reproach. What is the claret like? Blood.

On table six, the language of tongues is braised
in armagnac. The woman chewing suckling pig
must sleep with her husband later. Leg,
saddle and breast bleat against pure white cloth.

Alter *calf* to *veal* in four attempts. This is
the power of words; knife, tripe, lights, charcuterie.
A fat man orders his *rare* and a fine sweat
bastes his face. There are napkins to wipe the evidence

and sauces to gag the groans of abattoirs. The menu
lists the recent dead in French, from which they order
offal, poultry, fish. Meat flops in the jowls. Belch.
Death moves in the bowels. You are what you eat.

AND THEN WHAT

Then with their hands they would break bread
wave choke phone thump thread

Then with their tired hands slump
at a table holding their head

Then with glad hands hold other hands
or stroke brief flesh in a kind bed

Then with their hands on the shovel
they would bury their dead.

LETTERS FROM DEADMEN

Beneath the earth a perfect femur glows. I recall
a little pain and then a century of dust. Observe my anniversary,
place purple violets tenderly before the urn. You must.
No one can hear the mulching of the heart, which thrummed
with blood or drummed with love. Perhaps, by now,
your sadness will be less. Unless you still remember me.

I flung silver pigeons to grey air with secret messages
for men I had not met. Do they ever mention me
at work and was there weeping in the crematorium?
Dear wife, dear child, I hope you leave my room
exactly as it was. The pipe, the wireless and, of course,
the cricket photographs. They say we rest in peace.

Ash or loam. Scattered or slowly nagged by worms. I lie
above my parents in the family plot and I fit neatly
in a metal cask in ever-loving memory of myself.
They parted his garments, casting lots upon them
what every man should take. A crate of stout.
Small talk above the salmon sandwiches. Insurance men.

But here you cannot think. The voice-box imitates
the skeletons of leaves. Words snail imperceptibly and soundless
in the soil. Dear love, remember me. Give me biography
beyond these simple dates. Were there psalms and hired
    limousines?
All this eternally before my final breath and may
this find you as it leaves me here. Eventually.

WIDENER UNIVERSITY WOLFGRAM LIBRARY CHESTER PA